637
Lee

Leeper, Angela.
Dairy plant

NOV 0 6		
APR 0 2 2010		
MAY 2 1 2010		
OCT 0 3 2010		
OCT 2 8 2013		
MAY 1 6 2014		
NOV 3 2016		
NOV 1 8 2016		
NOV 3 0 2016		
JAN 3 0 2017		
FEB 2 4 2017		
APR 1 4 2017		
OCT 1 3 2017		
MAR 1 5 2019		
APR - 5 2019		

AR 2.3
0.5

Field Trip!

Dairy Plant

Angela Leeper

Heinemann Library
Chicago, Illinois

Designed by Kim Kovalick, Heinemann Library; Page layout by Que-Net Media
Printed and bound in China by South China Printing Company Limited.
Photo research by Jill Birschbach
08 07 06 05 04
10 9 8 7 6 5 4 3 2 1

Library of Congress Cataloging-in-Publication Data
Leeper, Angela.
  Dairy Plant / Angela Leeper
      p. cm. – (Field trip!)
Includes index.
Summary: An introduction to the workings of a dairy plant, from the milking of cows to the bottling of milk and the processing of other milk products.
  ISBN 1-4034-5160-5 (HC) 1-4034-5166-4 (Pbk.)
  1. Dairying–Juvenile literature. 2. Milk–Juvenile literature. 3.
  Dairy products–Juvenile literature. [1. Dairying. 2. Milk. 3. Dairy products.] I. Title.
  SF239.5.L44 2004
  637'.1–dc22

                                        2003014522

Acknowledgments
The author and publishers are grateful to the following for permission to reproduce copyright material:
p. 4 Robert Lifson/Heinemann Library; p. 5 Mazimilian Stock, Ltd./AGStockUSA; p. 6 Wolfgang Hoffmann/AGStockUSA; p. 7 Jeff Greenberg/PhotoEdit, Inc.; pp. 8, 9 Mark Turner/MidwestStock Photos; pp. 10, 11, 12, 17, 18, 19, 20, 21 Greg Williams/Heinemann Library; p. 13 Mark Richards/PhotoEdit, Inc.; p. 14 Bettmann/Corbis; p. 15 Macduff Everton/Corbis; p. 16 Patti McConville/MidWestStock Photos; p. 23 (T-B) Macduff Everton/Corbis, Craig Hutchins/Eye Ubiquitous/Corbis, Lester V. Bergman/Corbis, Maximillian Stock, Ltd./AGStockUSA, Greg Williams/Heinemann Library, Mark Turner/MidwestStock Photos; back cover (L-R) Wolfgang Hoffmann/AGStockUSA, Greg Williams/Heinemann Library

Cover photograph by David Young-Wolff/Photo Edit

Every effort has been made to contact copyright holders of any material reproduced in this book. Any omissions will be rectified in subsequent printings if notice is given to the publisher.

Special thanks to our advisory panel for their help in the preparation of this book:

Alice Bethke   Malena Bisanti-Wall   Ellen Dolmetsch, MLS
Library Consultant   Media Specialist   Tower Hill School
Palo Alto, California   American Heritage Academy   Wilmington, Delaware
                              Canton, Georgia

Special thanks to Maple View Farm and William Klein at Babcock Hall Dairy Plant, University of Wisconsin, Madison.

Contents

Some words are shown in bold, **like this.**
You can find them in the picture glossary on page 23.

Where Does Milk Come From?

We drink many kinds of milk, such as whole milk and chocolate milk.

We also eat butter, cheese, and ice cream.

All of these foods are **milk products.**

A dairy plant is a place where milk products are made.

Where Does the Dairy Plant Get the Milk From?

Milk comes from cows.

Baby cows suck milk from their mothers.

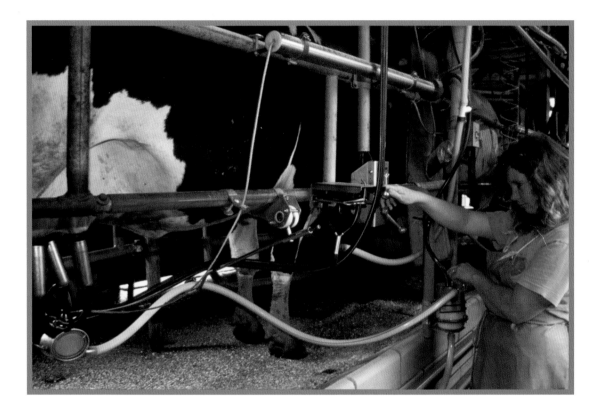

Farmers milk cows at a farm.

A milking machine sucks milk
like a baby cow.

How Does the Milk Get to the Dairy Plant?

The milk goes into a **tanker truck**.

The tanker truck brings the milk to the dairy plant.

What Happens to Milk at the Dairy Plant?

The milk goes through different machines.

A dairy worker checks the machines.

This machine heats up the milk and then cools it quickly.

This gets rid of **germs** in the milk and makes it safe to drink.

How Does Milk Get in the Bottles?

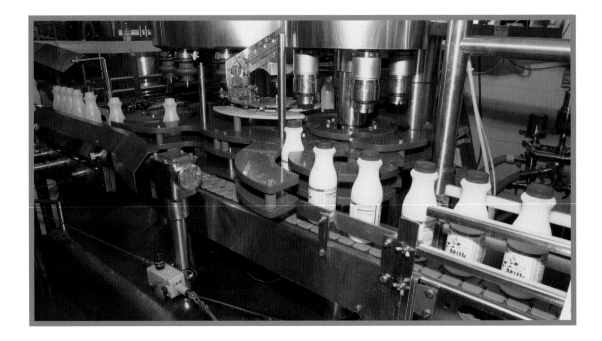

This machine fills the bottles with milk.

Some milk goes in cartons or jugs, too.

A dairy worker puts the milk
in a cold room.

Later, the milk goes to
grocery stores.

How Do They Make Butter?

AUGUST.

Butter is made from the part of milk called **cream.**

The cream is **churned** to make it thick.

People used to churn butter by hand.

Churning stirs the cream quickly and makes it solid.

Today, a big machine churns the butter.

How Do They Make Cheese?

curds

First, milk is heated.

Part of the milk turns into lumps called curds.

The curds are used to make cheese.

This cheese goes into **molds** to give it a round shape.

How Do They Make Ice Cream?

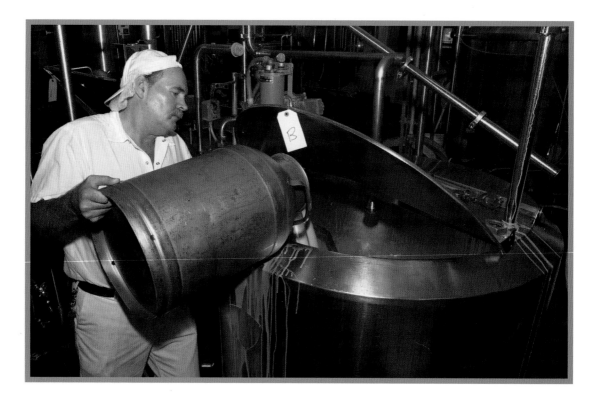

Ice cream is made with milk, **cream**, and sugar.

A dairy worker puts the ingredients in a big mixer.

A freezer makes the ice cream cold.

Then, a dairy worker puts the ice cream in containers.

What Happens to the Ice Cream Next?

A dairy worker puts the ice cream in a big freezer to keep it cold.

Later, the ice cream goes to grocery stores.

You may taste the ice cream at the dairy plant!

What is your favorite flavor?

Dairy Plant Map

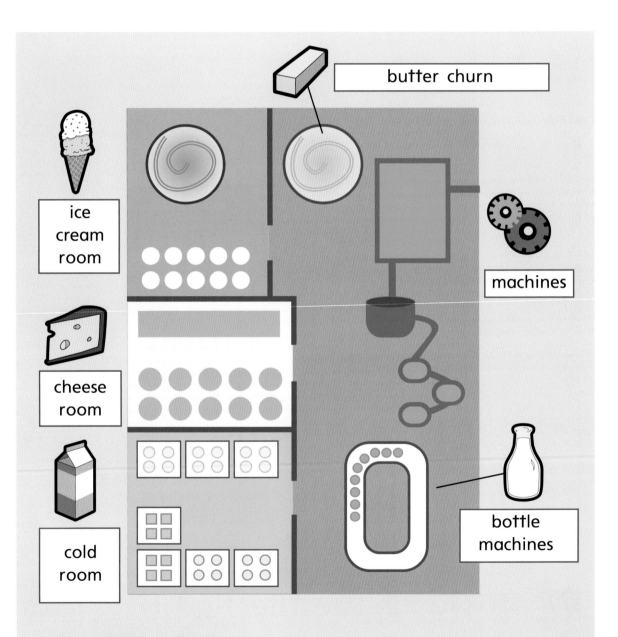

butter churn

ice cream room

machines

cheese room

cold room

bottle machines

22

Picture Glossary

churn
pages 14, 15
to turn something quickly

cream
pages 14, 15, 18
fatty part of milk

germ
page 11
small living thing that can cause sickness

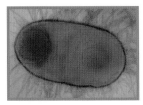
milk product
page 5
something made from milk, like butter and cheese

mold
page 17
container that gives something a shape

tanker truck
pages 8, 9
big truck that can carry liquids

Note to Parents and Teachers

Reading for information is an important part of a child's literacy development. Learning begins with a question about something. Help children think of themselves as investigators and researchers by encouraging their questions about the world around them. Each chapter in this book begins with a question. Read the question together. Look at the pictures. Talk about what you think the answer might be. Then read the text to find out if your predictions were correct. Think of other questions you could ask about the topic, and discuss where you might find the answers. Assist children in using the picture glossary and the index to practice new vocabulary and research skills.

Index